Shoes in the Night

by Russell Ginns
illustrated by David Gordon

© 2020 Sandviks, HOP, Inc. All Rights Reserved.

No part of this publication may be reproduced, stored in any retrieval system or transmitted, in any form or by any means, electronic, mechanical or otherwise, without prior written permission of the publisher.

Printed in China.

After the sun begins to set
And shadows start to creep,
I brush my teeth and get in bed,
But I can never sleep.

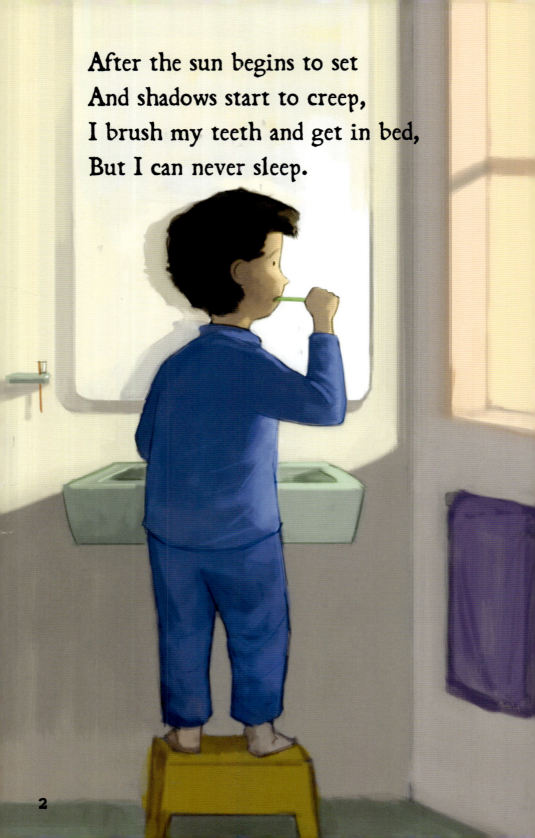

I close my eyes and breathe in deep,
And then I count to ten
Because I know that very soon
It all will start again.

The house is still and quiet.
You could hear a dropping pin.
Then, after just a moment,
THEY start creeping in.

The hinges on the front door creak,
And soon I hear them crawl.
First there's a bump and then a thump.
The boots are in the hall!

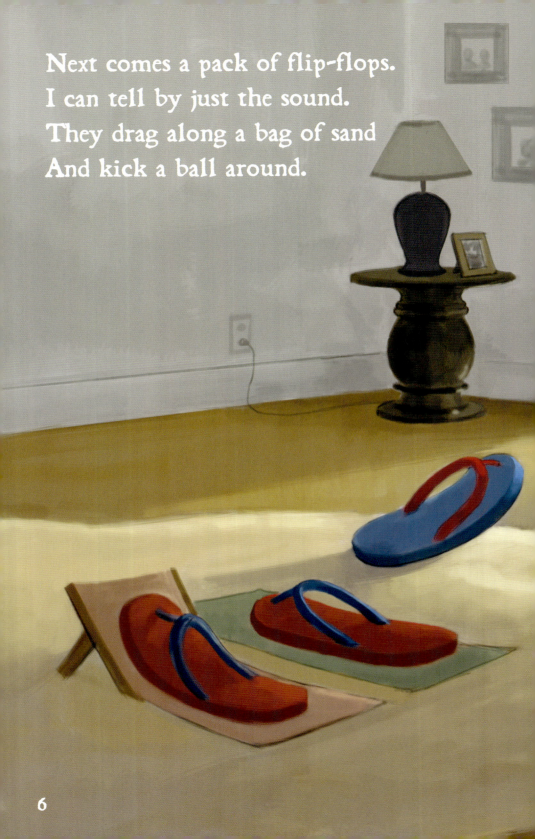

Next comes a pack of flip-flops.
I can tell by just the sound.
They drag along a bag of sand
And kick a ball around.

I hear the squishing of a sponge.
Plates rattle, glasses clink.
I bet a band of pumps and clogs
Are in the kitchen sink.

I hear some of them jumping.
They skip around a rope.
It sounds like they are having fun,
But do I like it? Nope!

And then strange music starts to play.
It happens every night.
Loud bumping, thumping,
banging, clanging—
This is just not right!

What could those shoes be up to?
What's making all that sound?
I get up out of bed,
And I start to snoop around.

I have to take a look down there.
I have to take a peek.
I slowly tiptoe down the stairs
And hope the stairs don't squeak.

Look! It's a great big party.
They've all come here to play.
I count at least a dozen shoes,
And more are on the way.

They hop on chairs. They kick in pairs.
They seesaw, skip, and prance.
One plays a drum, some sing, some hum,
While others swing and dance.

Then one shoe slips and then one trips.
They all begin to bump.
As each boot knocks another,
They fall in one big clump.

A cowboy boot is twisted.
A pump has lost its heel.
Three sneakers are all tangled.
They moan and groan and squeal.

When I see the battered boots,
I gasp a bit too loud.
Now I am face to face
With every shoe that's in the crowd.

There is no time to stop and think.
There is no time for fear.
I charge right in and go to work.
It's good that I am here.

I push a boot back into shape.
I fix a broken heel.
I help untwist some laces.
Oh, how good I feel!

The shoes all cheer. They stomp and clap,
So happy that I'm there.
Tonight I am a hero.
They lift me in the air.

So when the sun starts setting,
And shadows start to creep . . .

I race downstairs to play
With all my friends before I sleep!